MW00651934

Co-published by China Institute and EastBridge

125 East 65th Street New York New York 10021 USA
chinainstitute.org

Editor: Nancy Jervis
Photographic prints: Bernard Handzel
Gamble chronology and map research: Wayne W. J. Xing
Design: Chun-wo Pat, Whitespace Integrated Design, Inc.

Released in conjunction with the exhibition:
China Between Revolutions Revisited
China Institute
June 2004–July 2004
Co-organizers: Nancy Jervis and France Pepper
Curator: Nancy Jervis
Photographic prints: Bernard Handzel
Translation: Dawn Chen and Yin Hui

This publication is made possible through the generous support of The Sidney D. Gamble Foundation for China Studies.

Cover:
Gamble on Wheelbarrow.
Xundu to Chengdu, 1917

ISBN 1-891936-92-1

Distributed worldwide by EastBridge
64 Wall Street Norwalk CT 06850 USA
eastbridgebooks.org

MANUFACTURED IN THE UNITED STATES OF AMERICA

Abbreviations:
Peking: A Social Survey=P:SS
Ting Hsien: A North China Rural Community=TH:NCRC

Sidney Gamble's China
Revisited

千里來參國是
權憲法見精神
生事業千
古雲

Sidney
Photographs by
Gamble's
Sidney D. Gamble
China
from 1917 to 1931
Revisited

Edited by Nancy Jervis
Introduction by Jonathan D. Spence

CHINA INSTITUTE · EASTBRIDGE

Foreword:

One day in July, 2003, I opened up the New York Times to see stark images of industrial workers in today's China by a Chinese photographer named Zhou Hai. I was struck by two images in particular: one was of a worker, perhaps a steel worker, the other, almost certainly of a coal miner, caused me at once to think back to photographs taken by Sidney D. Gamble in the early twentieth century. I was quite familiar with these, having been curator of the exhibition *China Between Revolutions: Photographs by Sidney D. Gamble, 1917–1927* in 1989. The Gamble photographs were also striking yet un-prettied images of the way people lived and worked in China, albeit China in a different era. Some elements in all the photographs were quite similar: the hard work, for instance, that was taken for granted, and the intimate relationship of each photographer to his subject was something held in common. Still other elements were quite different: handicraft production, for example, had given way to heavy industry. It occurred to me that by placing contemporary images of China against the backdrop provided by Gamble's photographs, we could see for ourselves the remarkable transformation that had been wrought in China during the twentieth century.

Detail of *Fortuneteller, Hangzhou 1918*, p.111

The photographs in this exhibition and volume were selected from the approximately five thousand images in the Gamble collection with two goals in mind: they were to be representative of the collection as a whole, and had to provide a context for today's China as depicted by contemporary Chinese photographers. This latter goal reflects the significance of both the photographic collection and the whole body of Gamble's work, encompassing as it does five published books and three hours of film. Sidney Gamble was one of the first empirical social scientists and took many of his pictures to illustrate his research—Gamble's books were already considered classics in the China field well before his photographic archive was discovered by his daughter.

During the era in which Sidney Gamble took these photographs China was indeed a vastly different place from today. The Imperial era had recently ended in 1911 with the fall of the Qing (Manchu) dynasty. The Republican period that followed was chaotic: necessary social reforms began to be instituted for the first time, the May Fourth Movement of 1919 saw the beginnings of a national consciousness, and the Communist Party arose and ultimately won the struggle for hegemony in 1949.

As China continues its rapid transformation in the post-Mao era, the visual and written record provided by Gamble gains in importance. Gamble's extensive quantitative and qualitative research provides us with a baseline against which to measure the profound and rapid changes which China is still undergoing. In his works on the city of Beijing, *Peking: A Social Survey* (1921) and *How Chinese Families Live in Peiping* (1933), for example, Gamble documents the city in great detail, including everything from the waterworks system and the number of rickshaw pullers, to the education system, prison reform, and religion. At the same time, we can see from his images how elements of the culture and society had retained their continuity with the past.

Gamble continued to use his sharp eye and scientific methodology when he moved on to study the north China countryside in the 1930s. Based at James Yen's Rural Reconstruction site in Dingxian in Hebei province north of Beijing (see Jonathan Spence's Introduction), Gamble conducted the first studies in English of social and economic conditions in that region. Gamble's *Ting Hsien, A North China Rural Community* (1954) and *North China Villages: Social, Political and Economic Activities Before 1933* (1963) remain starting points for anthropologists and social historians seeking to measure the enormous changes that took place in the Chinese countryside during the twentieth century.

Fortuneteller, Hangzhou 1918
Fortunetellers were often consulted in planning weddings and funerals, and in choosing the site for a new house or a place of burial.

Although Gamble's books have been available in libraries, it is only since the 1980s that the public has been able to view the photographs and film footage in this remarkable archive. We owe this discovery to Sidney Gamble's daughter, Catherine Gamble Curran. She not only discovered the archive, but knew immediately that it should be brought to public view and promptly arranged to do so. She eloquently describes the circumstances of this discovery and the voyages of the photographs in her preface to this volume. Although Gamble recorded many of the images to illustrate his research, the photographic record he produced stands on its own. He depicted people and a way of life in a sympathetic and scholarly way unique in the annals of photography in China.

NANCY JERVIS
CHINA INSTITUTE · NEW YORK CITY
MAY 2004

S.D.G.

Preface:

THE REDISCOVERY OF THE SIDNEY D. GAMBLE photographic archive came about almost by accident and through a series of quite extraordinary coincidences. Of course, as we were growing up, my two sisters, my brother and I were well aware of our father's interest in photography. Family expeditions would see him draped about with cameras and light meters, and one or the other of us was often delegated, not without protest, to help carry some of the equipment. The large Graflex in its thick, square leather case that features prominently in one of the photographs in this book was still in use, and very heavy it was, too. The annual ritual of the taking of the Christmas card picture was one that we underwent without, perhaps, as good grace as we might have shown. I have vivid memories of my father in the library at home, surrounded by piles of papers, slide rule in hand, as he worked on his books or, at his big desk, turning the wheels of his splicing machine. And of course I had leafed through his books and glanced at the photographic illustrations but hadn't the experience or the knowledge to realize what a priceless legacy they represent.

Detail of *Gamble on Wheelbarrow, Xundu to Chengdu, 1917*, p.vi

So it came as a complete surprise some years ago when I was attending a meeting in Princeton, New Jersey, to see projected on a wall some beautiful although strangely-colored transparencies of Chinese scenes identified as having been taken by my father. The recently appointed executive director of Princeton-in-Asia, an organization dear to my father's heart and on whose board of trustees both my daughter and I now serve, had been looking into its history and had repeatedly come across my father's name. He made an appointment to talk to my mother and, during the interview, was directed by her to a closet on the third floor of the house where he found rosewood boxes containing several hundred hand-colored glass slides and shoe boxes stuffed with what turned out to be nearly six thousand black and white negatives. Shortly thereafter, curiosity led me to the same closet.

Gamble on Wheelbarrow, Xundu to Chengdu, 1917

The memory of the moment, now almost twenty years ago, when I first opened one of the rosewood boxes, took out a glass slide and held it up against the light is still vivid. There was no way that I could have known then that I had taken the first small step on a very long road that would lead eventually to Beijing, the city where my father spent so many happy and productive years and where I was born. Along that road I have had many adventures, made many discoveries and formed many friendships. Time and again, a chance word or a coincidence has led me to just the person who had the experience and expertise I needed at that particular moment. An introduction to the director of the Smithsonian Institution Traveling Exhibition Service made possible the first exhibition of Sidney Gamble's photographs that opened at China Institute in New York in 1989 and subsequently traveled to nineteen museums in the United States and Canada. I visited many of the venues and noticed, each time, the numbers of Chinese who were there. It was especially moving to see older men and women, undoubtedly grandparents, carefully explaining the different scenes to young children. Gradually, the "impossible dream" of taking Sidney Gamble's photographs back to China began to take shape in my imagination.

Once again, it seemed that fate intervened to make my dream a reality. I was put in touch with the formidable Ms. Hai Di of the Beijing Haiyin Arts and

Culture Co., Ltd. She secured the necessary permit from the Ministry of Culture and, by great good fortune, was able to book space in September of 1999 in the vast halls of the Museum of Chinese History on Tiananmen Square. There was, however, one caveat. Because our opening date, September 11th, was so close to that which would mark the celebration of the fiftieth anniversary of the founding of the People's Republic, we would have to have special permission from the Central Committee of the Communist Party! This was maddeningly and rather worryingly slow in coming. But I convinced myself that destiny was still on our side and said nothing to the jolly group of twenty-four, family, friends and colleagues, who gathered in Beijing for a few days of sight-seeing, shopping and dining before the scheduled opening. Of course, they soon found out, but we crossed our fingers and enjoyed being treated as celebrities, appearing daily in the local Chinese and English language press and nightly on television. Exactly forty-eight hours before the deadline, permission came through! The exhibition, which comprised two hundred and ten images, subsequently traveled to fourteen cities on the Chinese mainland and to Hong Kong and was seen by over a million people.

And now the wheel has come full circle. Sidney Gamble's photographs have come home to China Institute where they were first shown fifteen years ago—almost to the day! The traumatic events of Tiananmen Square exploded just before the scheduled opening day in June of 1989. We discussed whether or not we should postpone the event but, in the end, we decided to proceed as planned. I like to think that Sidney Gamble's photographs might have been a source of some reassurance to those who love China and the indomitable Chinese people.

None of the three exhibitions could have taken place without the extraordinary efforts and dedication of the following: Nancy Jervis, distinguished scholar and China expert, Vice President and Director of Programs for China Institute, who, from the very beginning, had the vision to see what the possibilities were and who has remained a staunch friend, supporter and trusted advisor during all these years. In addition to all of her other responsibilities she has, with immense generosity and consummate professionalism, undertaken the complex and time consuming task of supervising every detail of *China Between Revolutions Revisited*, from helping to choose images down to the translation of the labels; Wayne W. J. Xing, Director of China Programs, Sidney D. Gamble Foundation, historian, researcher, translator, courier, facilitator and tireless team member whose enthusiastic devotion to Sidney Gamble has helped to overcome all difficulties; Bernard Handzel, whose love of the photographs and whose deep appreciation of their artistic value and historical importance has inspired him not only to perform miracles in the darkroom, but also to volunteer his help, support and valued advice whenever needed. The friendship of these, my associates and colleagues, has truly enriched my life.

The list of those who have helped to make my "impossible dream" come true is long and my gratitude extends to many, first and foremost to the members of my family who have so generously funded the project from the beginning: my mother, Elizabeth Lowe Gamble; my sister and brother-in-law, Louise Gamble Harper and Theodore Schuchat; my brother and sister-in-law, David Lowe Gamble, now deceased, and Regitze Gamble; my children and their spouses, Constance and Roemer McPhee and Peter and Bonni Curran; my nephews, Alan Burnett Harper, Todd Edward Harper, James Gamble Harper, David Baker Gamble, Christopher Lee Gamble, Stephen Lowe Symchych; my nieces, Kimberly Gamble and Christine Symchych; and to the trustees and the members of the Advisory Board of the Sidney D. Gamble Foundation for China Studies: Peter G. Curran, Constance C. McPhee, Theodore Schuchat, Peggy Blumenthal, Marcia M. Curran, Robert T. Curran, John C. Evans, Louise G. Harper, Yien Koo King, Richard S. Lanier, Douglas P. Murray, Robert B. Oxnam, Richard H. Ritter, now deceased, Datus C. Smith, Jr., now deceased, Pallavi Shah, Jonathan D. Spence, Mildred A. Talbot and Phillips Talbot. Through their knowledge of China, their affection for my father and their admiration for his work, they have contributed in ways too numerous to mention here.

Special thanks are due to the following: to Jonathan D. Spence, John Hersey and Carrington Goodrich for writing with such insight and appreciation about my father and the China he knew; to Robert B. Oxnam, past President of the Asia Society and China scholar, whose genuine and contagious admiration of my father's work encouraged me from the beginning and who persuaded Jonathan Spence to make that first trip down from New Haven to see the albums; to Nicholas Platt, Vishakha Desai, Carol Herring and Julie Lang of the Asia Society who take such obvious pride and pleasure in the Society's permanent display of some of the treasures of the collection; to Maria Morris Hambourg of the Metropolitan Museum of Art and Valrae Reynolds of the Newark Museum for their many helpful suggestions and introductions; to Raye Farr and Sue Williams for undertaking the editing and preservation of the movie film; to Margaret Riggs Buckwater for her meticulous cataloguing; to Martha Lund Smalley, Archivist of the Yale Divinity School Library, for making available my father's papers; to Paula Webster for the enthusiastic expertise with which she has handled relations with the press and public; to Madelyn Latimer for her patience and perseverance, for her ability to keep the cast of characters straight and to locate whatever it is that is needed at any time; to

Elizabeth Brantley Turner who understands spread sheets as well as photography; to Jason Eyster for going up to that third floor closet in the first instance and, finally, to the many friends, among them Patty Tang, Mary Pei, Sarina Tang, Annping Chin, Beverley Jackson, T. C. Hsu, Robert Armstrong, Terrill Lautz, Jerome A. Cohen, Christophe W. Mao, Ken Winter, Teri Edelstein, Nini and Robin Murray-Phillipson and Helen and John Bachofen whose interest and enthusiasm have sustained and encouraged me. I have especially enjoyed a lively correspondence with Mrs. Anne Goodrich and Dr. Richard H. Ritter, now deceased, contemporaries of my father, family friends and "old China hands" who have, with such charming generosity, shared with me their memories of my father and of China.

I am especially indebted to the trustees and staffs of the Luce Foundation and the Starr Foundation whose early financial support convinced me that this was a project worth pursuing.

My most profound gratitude and that of all the members of the Gamble family is due to the Beijing Haiyin Arts and Culture Co., Ltd. and to its director, Ms. Hai Di. Her faith, courage, trust and friendship made it possible to show to the new China these images of the old China that Sidney Gamble loved so well.

I am especially grateful to Jack Maisano, President of China Institute, and to France Pepper, Associate Director of Public Programs, who has given so generously of their time and energies and have met every looming deadline in order to make *China Between Revolutions Revisited* a reality. My thanks go to Elizabeth Kim and to Willow Hai Chang, also of China Institute, for their invaluable help and cooperation; to Chun-wo Pat, who designed this beautiful book, and to Doug Merwin and Joe West of EastBridge Books, who so generously offered to distribute the book; to Robyn Liverant for her excellent public relations work and to Paula Webster for still being there; to Dawn Chen and Yin Hui for their expert translations. Time was short, but thanks to everyone's enthusiastic help and support, Sidney Gamble's extraordinary photographs are once again on view.

There is an old saying: "It is a wise child that knows its own father." I think and hope that I am wiser now than I was. I have looked at China through my father's eyes and through the eye of his camera. I have shared his youthful enthusiasms and his joys of discovery, appreciated his quiet humor, admired his persistence and determination and been moved by his idealism and humanity. I shall always be grateful for having had this opportunity.

CATHERINE GAMBLE CURRAN
NEW YORK CITY
MAY 2004

自古皆有死可恨壯志未酬
中原憑誰挽
大地竟何之
卅年來排滿興中
功不妨一去

Introduction:

FOR THOSE OF US TUGGED CONSTANTLY by a continuing need to try to understand the dynamics of China's past—and the promise of her future—any witness to lost moods and events is valuable. Sidney D. Gamble is especially helpful since he came at China from three different perspectives out of which he somehow managed to fashion a coherent unity. The three were, first, his deep conviction of the relevance of Christian teaching to China's plight; second, his training in social sciences and economics, which enabled him to accumulate the data that would engender creative changes; and third, his love of photography, which would add the camera's eye to his own effort to focus on the crisis of his time.

Detail of *Sun Yat-sen Funeral Scrolls, Beijing 1925*, p.67

As if that were not enough to attract our interest, Sidney D. Gamble's four sojourns in China—in 1908, 1917–1919, 1924–27 and 1931–1932 were during times of unusual turmoil, drama and excitement. The first journey took an eighteen-year old in 1908 to Qing-dynasty Hangzhou on a family visit with his parents. Though we know very little of this first visit, Hangzhou must have seemed a dream-like vision of timeless China to the travelers, with its hills, woods, and villas encircling China's most famous scenic lake. And with the Gambles' Hangzhou host being himself a serious enthusiast of photography, young Sidney must have had a fine introduction to the opportunities that China offered to the collector of images.

Clear now to historians, but surely shrouded from view at the time, was the fact that the Qing dynasty was doomed, by internal weakness, dissension, and foreign pressures, to a speedy collapse. Both the Empress Dowager and the reform-minded but politically inept Guangxu emperor died in that same year of 1908, leaving the country's future in the hands of an infant emperor and his Manchu regents. By February 1912 as Sidney entered his last year at

1898	1899–1900	c.1906
Hundred Days of Reform	Boxer Uprising	Approximately 1,300 Chinese students study in Japan

Princeton, the Qing emperor was forced to abdicate, and China's fate was left to the untried institutions of a fledgling republic, the politically inexperienced associates of Sun Yat-sen's revolutionary organizations, and the ambitious military commanders scattered across China's provinces.

By 1908 the province of Zhejiang, in which Hangzhou was located, was a center of radical political activity in which a host of new Western ideas, including socialism, anarchism, and social-Darwinism, were exciting young intellectuals to strike at the foundations of the Qing state, through both the constitutional forms of local provincial assemblies and the extra-legal means of inflammatory polemical literature and political assassinations. How little this process could be understood in Zhejiang by the local villagers and townspeople, intent on the routines of their own daily lives, has been caught for all time in what is perhaps the greatest of China's modern short stories, "The True Story of Ah Q," written by the Zhejiang-born Lu Xun in 1921.

By the time this subtle yet bitter indictment of the Chinese people's inability to understand the nature of their political and cultural predicament had appeared, Sidney Gamble had already made his second sojourn in China, from 1917 to 1919. This journey began with an adventurous photographic expedition in the company of his friends up the Yangzi River, through the rapids above Yichang to Chongqing in Sichuan province. The excitement of such a journey and the terrible strain on the coolie laborers hauling the heavy boats against the swift currents were later to be indelibly caught by another young American visitor to China, John Hersey, in his novel *A Single Pebble.* Sidney Gamble was then learning to use his camera as well as his words, and his friends recalled how he lugged around his "big, ungainly camera" on all occasions, while Gamble himself, processing his own negatives along the way, as any serious photographer of the time had to do, noted in a diary entry how seventeen full loads of water were needed at a time to develop and wash the film.

Sidney D. Gamble and His Smith Corona, 1917
The sedan chair was a common form of transportation in the Chinese hinterland. When Gamble and his two friends traveled up the Yangzi River into Sichuan province, 15 coolies carried them and their 17 pieces of baggage.

It took fifteen chair-coolies to carry the small group of travelers and their seventeen pieces of baggage. No westerners—an more than any Chinese of even modest means—would have thought of tramping the dusty tracks on their own two feet in those days. Surely it is to this trek through Sichuan that the wonderful photo of Sidney

1908

Death of the Empress Dowager and the emperor Guangxu

1911

October: Qing dynasty overthrown

1912

January 1: Sun Yat-sen inaugurates the Chinese Republic in Nanjing; Yuan Shikai becomes its first President

D. Gamble belongs, the one showing him perched on his bamboo shoulder chair, a sun-proof canopy over his head, a wide-brim hat pulled rakishly down over his sunglasses, his fingers poised above the typewriter balanced on a little stand beside his knees. It is as fine a vision of a Western scholar in action during field work as has survived in any photograph collection.

For Gamble was now a fledgling scholar, and poised to become a fine one. After his graduation from Princeton in 1912, he had worked for a time in California and then entered graduate school at the University of California at Berkeley to work in economics. As if anticipating the demands of his future work in China, he not only studied labor and industrial economics but also worked with the California State Commission on Immigration and Housing. Further deepening his understanding of group dynamics and social deprivation, he spent six months on a fellowship working at a reform school for delinquent boys.

Upon finishing his Sichuanese travels, Gamble went to Beijing in response to the call of fellow Princetonian John Stewart Burgess, '05, who wanted Gamble to make a social survey of the life of the ordinary residents of the city. This information, it was hoped, would both help the YMCA in its day-to-day work and enable the Princeton men connected with the Y to make responsible suggestions for social reform to the local political leaders.

One problem here was that the political system of China had fallen into a position of near-anarchy since the Qing collapse of 1912. The nominal constitutional assembly in Beijing was only a rump group from which most of the once-legally elected members bad been purged, or else had resigned. The presidents and premiers who succeeded each other in swift succession often had little or no interest in democratic institutions and were easily manipulated, terrorized, or corrupted by the various generals who, in turn, controlled the various sub-regions into which north China and Manchuria had fragmented.

It was in 1917, the year of Gamble's return to China, that the gesture of entering the World War in Europe on the Franco-British side had been made by the Chinese government. Some two hundred thousand coolies had been dispatched to Europe to help the Allies with transportation and construction projects, work that would free up able-bodied European troops to be sent to the trenches to face the Germans. In this turbulent European world, members of the YMCA were active, as in China, helping to analyze the Chinese workers' social problems, teaching Mass Education courses to try to break the hold of the illiteracy in which nearly all such impoverished men were trapped, and introducing elements of Western democratic thought to help them attain greater dignity.

Those governing China had not joined the allied cause out of altruism they hoped, by this act, to win support for their attempt to regain all the Chinese

1912

General reform of the education system and the founding of Beijing University

1915

Japan imposes the Twenty-one Demands

1915

Publication of New Youth (*Xin Qing Nian*) marks the beginning of the New Culture Movement

territories that had been seized or "leased" by Germany during the previous two decades of aggressive foreign imperialism. Unknown to the Chinese politicians, however, a series of secret agreements between Britain, France and the United States with Japan, intended to keep Japan from allying with Germany, had, in effect, promised to Japan the very same territorial and economic privileges that had previously been held by Germany. When this news became apparent in May 1919, thousands of Chinese students and townspeople, in Beijing and elsewhere, reacted with furious protests and demonstrations, blaming their political leaders for ineptitude or betrayal and the foreign powers for their deceit and greed. Beijing during this period was a stormy, excited place, and Gamble was able, in some unsurpassed photographs, to catch on film the exasperated young people's mood of anger and despair.

While Gamble witnessed these events, he carried on his work at the YMCA—from which he drew no salary, needing none as a descendant of one of the founders of Procter and Gamble—and acceded to Burgess' request that he compile a social survey of Beijing. Gamble was fortunate here in that his own training in survey-taking and economics coincided with a dramatic growth in enrollment at Beijing universities, so that large numbers of young Chinese were now interested in learning techniques of Western social science and applying them to the needs of their own society. With the assistance of such students and other helpers, and by his own hard work, Gamble slowly pieced together evidence from the workers in the city that would be tabulated in his first book, written with the assistance of John Stewart Burgess and published in 1921 as *Peking: A Social Survey*.

In his introduction to the book, Gamble made a careful attempt to state his views on the interconnection between the Christian message and the practical problems confronting China. He noted that many non-Christian Chinese were promoting social reforms at the same time that many fervent Christians were preaching God's word but failing to relate it to the needs of the country as a whole. Characteristically, after raising the problem succinctly, Gamble let a young Chinese speaker provide the voice for the rest of the argument:

> The right spirit and attitude are not alone sufficient to transform the nation. The spirit of love, the general social principles of Christianity and even the far-off aim of the Kingdom are desired by the young, intelligent future leaders of China, but they also demand that definite methods and processes be used in applying these new principles and realizing these new ideals. One young man who recently became a Christian joined the church with the belief that it was a group of men and women banded together with the purpose of bringing in a new social order founded on the principles laid down by Jesus Christ. Two

1916

Death of Yuan Shikai and beginning of the warlord period

1917

Bolshevik Revolution successful in Russia

1919–1921

John Dewey, invited by Hu Shih, lectures in China

months after he was baptized he came to the person who had introduced him to the pastor and said, "What sort of institution is this that you recommended to me rejoin? I thought you said it was a group of men and women whose main business it was to bring in the Kingdom of God in Peking It was with that object that I joined the church. I have been there now for two months and have done nothing but listen to sermons on Sunday! So far they have given me nothing to do!" The lack of a comprehensive Christian social program, pioneered by the church, is due not so much to definite neglect of this important field by the Chinese and foreign church leaders, as to the lack of accurate scientific knowledge of social conditions and methods of community service.

Gamble's carefully accumulated data on Beijing's population—incomes, health, recreation, occupations, and such important matters as police services and orphanage structures—were immediately appreciated by Western reviewers of the book, among them the philosopher John Dewey, just returned from his own extensive residence in Beijing. Dewey called Gamble's book "unquestionably the best social survey ever made from the Christian viewpoint in any foreign mission field," praised the range of topics it covered, and termed it "indispensable to further studies of China."

One important feature of the book was the inclusion of fifty photographs taken by Gamble of Beijing life and work. These photographs were selected from close to twenty-five hundred in all that he worked on and classified as he wrote the book back in the United States in 1920 and 1921. The photographs were especially impressive for their illumination of social problems: student demonstrators being led away under arrest; blind furniture makers weaving their rush chairs, eyes turned sightlessly inward; girl children recently saved from lives of slavery or prostitution, standing meekly in line, heads lowered, save for two lured by the attraction of Gamble's camera to peer cautiously in his direction; a beggar family of six destitute children and a single parent, where two older boys have obviously shared a single suit of clothes, one confident in the trousers, the other nervously looking sideways out of the picture in an open shirt that fails to shroud his growing genitals; a group of twenty prisoners in a cell fifteen-by-twenty feet in size, squinting at the sudden rush of light that signifies the jailer's acquiescence in the photographer's presence.

The quality, imaginativeness, technical level, and variety of these photographs deserve to lift Gamble from the ranks of the mere recorder of Chinese life and scenery and to place him among the selected few who truly used their cameras to catch the evanescent moment in which a particular face, a gesture, a juxtaposition of elements, comes to be more than itself and to speak for a whole time and culture.

1919	1921	1925
The May Fourth Movement, protesting the Treaty of Versailles, erupts in Beijing	Chinese Communist Party (CCP) founded in Shanghai	March 12: Sun Yat-sen dies in Beijing

According to Gamble's note, "This family might report, as one actually did, an annual expenditure of thirty cents for clothes." (P:SS, P.271)

Fine photography already had a distinguished tradition in China. As early as the 1860s, Felix Beato and John Thomson set the highest of standards with their portrayals of the tragedies of war and the ranges of Chinese facial types, occupations, and scenery. In the 1870s Saunders and Fisler dominated the Shanghai professional photographic world, as did Griffith in Hong Kong. By the end of the century the Empress Dowager herself had become an enthusiast of the photographic genre and let herself—often dramatically made-up in allegorical or religious guise—be photographed in the company of her favorite eunuchs and retainers. By the 1920s a generation of Chinese photographers had also mastered the genre, and moved confidently to begin recording their own country.

But Gamble's work stands on its own. In some of his photos—such as the one of the aged Chinese lady aristocrat [see page 53], with the bound feet in brocade shoes, smoking a cigarette through a long holder as her rimless eyeglasses slide down her nose—Gamble caught an image as arresting as any of those by his greatest successor in China, Henri Cartier-Bresson.

Returning to China in 1924, again under YMCA auspices and now married to Elizabeth Lowe, Sidney D. Gamble plunged once more into the task of analyzing and recording the central elements of Beijing life. This time he

1926

First Mass Education School opens

1926

Northern Expedition launched by CCP and KMT to defeat warlords

1926

China Institute founded in New York City by John Dewey, Paul Monroe and Hu Shih, with money from the Boxer Indemnity decided to focus on a smaller group of families and to follow their expenditures more closely. With a team of Chinese assistants to help him, he tracked the daily incomes and expenses of 283 families for an entire year. His classifications, which comprised thirty-seven major categories, were meticulous. He and his researchers related each family's income to its original place of birth and compared wages and consumption per unit, age, sex, occupation (fifty-five categories for men, fourteen for women), food types, clothing, rent, and utilities.

In addition to studying the urban lifestyles of Beijing families, Gamble had now adapted the more challenging goal of studying Chinese rural life. Some evaluations had already been attempted by Chinese researchers, and an ambitious venture was being developed by John Lossing Buck and his students in the countryside around Nanjing. Members of the Chinese Communist Party, which had been founded in 1921, were also eager to assess the true nature of rural life and rural suffering, so as to direct their activism towards the areas of greatest effectiveness and need. But Gamble himself at first found the times unpropitious for such a rural survey. China in 1925 was even more perilous than China in 1919—the civil war seemingly more ferocious, the economic demands of the warlords and their troops ever more rapacious. As Gamble noted in a letter of December 16, 1925:

> My own plans for research work in the country have been upset by the war. What with the seizing of carts, extra taxes, etc., the people are very fearful and would not be at all willing to give us the information needed for a rural survey. We have been able, however, to get at records in Peking. We have worked out the history of exchange between copper and silver since 1900. We have the figures for wages and the prices of grains and other commodities for the same period and are figuring out the rise and fall of the standard of living of the Peking working man.

So Gamble continued his urban work, but kept such a close eye on local rural realities and the details of warlord politics that his letters through 1925, 1926, and into late 1927, when he ended his third China-sojourn, form an important addition to our knowledge of China at the time. Not sympathetic to "the more radical element among the students" (letter of December 16, 1925), Gamble nevertheless discussed their activities and alleged motives with care, and, once again, he was very often there with his camera, catching the street scenes, the faces and gestures of the people. In a careful letter of February 18, 1926, he noted the arrival of thousands of wounded warlord troops in Beijing and its suburbs, of the absence of doctors and drugs to treat them, of the amputation made necessary for those wounded who, for lack of hospital space, were left to lie out in the bitter cold and suffer frostbite. Was it humanly right, Gamble

1927

KMT turns on Communists and workers in Shanghai

1927–1937

Archaeological excavations on the site of the Shang (1700–1027 BCE) capital near Anyang

1931

Mukden Incident: Japanese invade Manchuria

watched doctors argue, to amputate both the legs of a wounded man to "save his life" knowing what the life of a legless beggar would be in Beijing? And yet, as he observed in another vivid letter of June 1926, these same soldiers, once recovered, or their comrades-in-arms, caused agonies in the impoverished countryside around the city:

The Relief Committee at first planned to sell grain in the principal villages outside the city wall but this has not been possible as it has been found that even if people could buy the grain the soldiers would take it from them before they got it home. Because of the difficulty in getting food a great many people have had to refugee into the city. The newspapers have reported that as many as 400,000 refugees have come inside the walls, but this is very evidently a big exaggeration. In the refugee camps opened by the various philanthropic organizations they have been caring for about 15,000. Of course a great many more have friends or relatives in the city and are staying with them.

It is almost time for the wheat harvest and recent rains are tempting many of the refugees to go back to their farms but it looks as though they would not be able to gather much of the grain. In some places the horses of the army have been grazed in the wheat fields. From other villages we hear that the soldiers have demanded scythes so that they can cut the grain for themselves. The soldiers have put signs on some wheat fields saying that the grain must not be disturbed as it is for their use. It looks very much as though the countryside would be faced with famine before fall.

On occasion, Sidney Gamble's testimony echoed and complemented that of some of China's sharpest and most talented observers. An example is the shooting of more than forty student demonstrators by warlord troops on March 18, 1926, a massacre that included several of Lu Xun's own young women students from the Women's Normal College in Beijing. Lu Xun wrote a searingly beautiful elegy for three young people, so cruelly done to death, but Gamble himself showed how a Westerner's sympathy could also be caught and held. He had an unerring eye for the vivid detail, as in the penultimate sentence of his account in air April 20, 1926 letter:

The shooting of the students on March 18th was a terrible tragedy. After a meeting in front of the Forbidden City a group marched to the Cabinet office to protest against the ultimatum the foreign powers had given China concerning the closing of the Pei Ho at Taku. Many of them were the more conservative students, though the Kuomintang and the communists were represented in the parade. I passed the crowd on Hata Men Street. They were cheering but were more orderly than many of the demonstrations last May. Just how much the students threatened to use force at the Cabinet office we do

1933–1935

Japanese advance in northern China

1934

Communists begin the Long March. Chiang Kai-shek launches the New Life Movement

1935

Zunyi Conference re-establishes Mao Zedong as leader of the Communist Party

not know, but once the guard started firing they kept it up for fifteen or twenty minutes. The soldiers used their bayonets on the wounded and robbed the bodies of the dead, Even glasses were snatched from one of the girls as she was getting out through a back gate. Altogether forty-eight were killed or died of their wounds.

But even in the midst of all this field research, YMCA business, and human tragedy in city and countryside, there was room for family joys. Almost deadpan, though with deliberate rhetorical effect since the sentence comes shortly after the news of the student deaths and warlord outrages in 1926, Gamble closed the letter of April 20, 1926 with the sentence, "Her mother says that the arrival of Catherine Conover Gamble on March 21st is much more important than all this political news."

April and early May 1927, as Gamble noted alliteratively, was a time of "politics, propaganda, panic-rumor, riot, revolution, refugees" (letter of May 13, 1927). Few historians could disagree with this succinct and accurate summary of the period in which the forces of Chiang Kai-shek and his Shanghai allies turned on the communists and labor unions, killing thousands in the streets; when the communists in Hankou tried to unite with a splinter left-leaning group of Chiang's Kuomintang, and the troops of Manchurian warlord Zhang Zuolin broke into the Russian legation area in Beijing, seizing all the radical Chinese sheltering there and executing twenty or more after a court-martial trial.

In the Chinese countryside, nevertheless, attempts at mass education and land reform were underway, among the most impressive being the one at Dingxian in Hebei province, south of Beijing, directed by James Yen. Gamble found time to visit the area and to write enthusiastically about it in letters home He was especially struck by the interconnection of mass education with famine relief and could never resist commenting on the bustle, excitement and energy that always seemed to be such a vibrant part of Chinese life. As he put it in a letter of October 1, 1927:

The trip to Ting Hsien gave me a fine glimpse of country life as we were able to get into the villages and talk with many of the people. It was the busy season and we found a great many of the farmers irrigating, drawing water from the wells dug with the Famine Relief funds. In some places they use animals, but most of the water was being raised by man and woman power.

In one of the villages they were having a big temple fair. In the country districts there are some religious observances with the temple fairs but for the most part they are for buying and selling. it was a country holiday and crowds came from all around. The village streets were jammed and in the fields all around the merchants were displaying their wares, almost everything used in

1936

Death of the progressive writer Lu Xun

1937

Marco Polo Bridge Incident launches World War II

1942–1943

Famine in Henan kills an estimated 2 million people

country life, carts, timber, cattle, brushes, baskets for the wells, grain, wooden benches, cloths, iron ware. The Mass Education people had a big parade of their students, marching to the village stage where they gave a Mass Education play. I wish I could describe for you the sea of faces that crowded in under the mat shed roof. The people were packed so closely that from the stage they looked like nothing but faces. After the play the secretaries got the people to sing the Mass Education song, words set to a Chinese tune, and going home along the country roads we could hear the people singing the song. The experience of the first year of the country experiment of the Mass Education Association makes me feel that it is going to produce fine results, and I think we can hope for the development of a program that will add much to the life of the rural communities.

Back home in the United States by 1928, Gamble worked steadily with the statistics he had accumulated on the 283 Beijing families. The results were published in 1933 in the remarkable study *How Chinese Families Live in Peiping* (Beijing had ceased to be China's capital and was renamed Peiping). In the cases of illiterate families, Gamble had employed assistant scribes to help them complete the simple questionnaires he issued, and the results were a fine example of clear sociological analysis, figures, and commentary on the diets of the poor; for example, the bleak finding that the poorer families could afford no luxuries of any kind, not even vegetables, above a monthly figure of twenty-two cents a month, or fruit of any variety above a monthly total of fifteen cents. In all, Gamble tabulated food alone under an astonishing 310 headings and included detailed figures on clothes, housing, light, weddings and funerals, water, and "miscellaneous," which included the pitifully small outlays made for education, health, travel, objects of household use, and recreation. As in his first book, Gamble included haunting photographs of highest quality and effectiveness: water-sellers hefting their barrows, wayside urban shrines, the paper figures and mock-ups of American-style automobiles now burned to accompany the dead to their final resting places, and Chinese women wailing before the pyramid-like tombs of their deceased family members

During 1931 and 1932, while the volume was in its final stages, Gamble returned to China for his fourth and last sojourn. Once again, despite the apparent successes of Chiang Kai-shek's regime in uniting the country under his Kuomintang leadership, the outlook was bleak. A Japanese *coup d'état* in Manchuria led to the fall of the China-leaning regime there and the virtual consolidation of Japanese power. Japanese armed attacks on Shanghai resulted in immense Chinese sacrifices of life, of both troops and civilians. Sidney Gamble concentrated on working on details of the rural reforms being

1945

World W ar II ends, Civil War begins in China

1949

People's Republic of China proclaimed in Beijing on October 1

1953

Official Census counts 601 million inhabitants

attempted at Dingxian and on pondering the social and cultural effects of various well-meaning programs. Over the following years, this final visit to China led to three more remarkable studies.

Because of the exigencies of Gamble's own career, family, and the outbreak of World War II, *Ting Hsien: A North China Rural Community* did not appear until 1954. it was a rich and complex study, dealing with family, government, budgets, taxes, irrigation, farm operation, and the local industries in over four hundred rural families. The book included, though less persuasively and prominently than in the earlier urban volumes, a supplement of photographs of local faces, customs, and technology that enriched the study as a whole. In this volume Gamble revealed his endless intellectual curiosity by including a series of literal translations and summaries of the local dramas that gave such life to rural culture. At their most vivid, passages from this book showed a fresh vision of local political self-consciousness among the Chinese.

In 1963, when Gamble was seventy-three years old, he published a much broader study of northern rural China, detailed analyses of no less than eleven village communities which he entitled *North China Villages*. Again, the statistical information was full, the narrative lucid and informed, and the small supplement of photographs profoundly effective in its resonance and range: unforgettable were the naked boys and their hogs outside a village shrine; the woman traveler being pushed across country in a wheelbarrow by a tattered coolie; and an old temple pilgrim so deeply lined and worn that in her face one is tempted to read the whole history of China since Gamble's first visit in 1908, imprinted as on a mariner's chart [see page 54].

Gamble died in 1968 leaving behind his widow, four children and ten-now twelve-grandchildren, along with his four remarkable books. A fifth book, building on elements already presented in the third, was published posthumously in 1970 under the title *Chinese Village Plays from the Ting Hsien Region*. It remains an important addition to our knowledge of traditional Chinese folk culture.

Sidney D. Gamble's findings were open-minded, clear-headed, methodologically intelligent (though not always beyond criticism by scholars of different views), startlingly imaginative and—when presented in photographic form—vigorously ebullient, unsentimental, and starkly, yet never cruelly, illustrative of the deep and real suffering that lay at the heart of China's long revolution.

JONATHAN D. SPENCE
YALE UNIVERSITY · NEW HAVEN
1989

1958

The Great Leap Forward begins

1962

Death of the prominent May Fourth figure Hu Shih

1966

The Great Proletarian Cultural Revolution begins

S. D. G.

SIDNEY D. GAMBLE
1890–1968

CHRONOLOGY OF SIDNEY D. GAMBLE

1890

BORN on July 12 in Cincinnati, Ohio, to David Berry and Mary Huggins Gamble; grandson of James Gamble, who, with William Procter, founded Procter & Gamble in 1837.

1896–1907
Attended Miss Sattler's School and University School in Cincinnati, and Thacher School in Ojai, California.

1ST SOJOURN: 1908

1908
First sojourn in China. Traveled with parents to Hangzhou by way of Honolulu, Japan, and Korea.

1912
Graduated magna cum laude from Princeton University with a Bachelor of Literature degree; elected to Phi Beta Kappa.

1913–1914
Served as secretary and treasurer of Escondido Land and Town Company, San Diego, California.

2ND SOJOURN: 1917–1919

1916–1917
Arrived in China in May for second sojourn. Together with Robert Fitch and J. H. Arthur, traveled up the Yangzi River, from Zhejiang province deep into Sichuan province, taking numerous photographs.

1918 SPRING
Visited flood relief camps in Tianjin and traveled to Beijing. Traveled with G. Sherwood Eddy to Xiamen, Fuzhou, Ningbo, Hong Kong, and Manila. Joined the international staff of the YMCA in Beijing and became a member of Princeton University Center in China (Princeton Court).

1918 SUMMER
Visited Beidaihe and Bei Niu Ding (Hebei).

1918 FALL
Conducted field-work for a social survey of Beijing with John Stewart Burgess while teaching elementary economics and the principles of philanthropic and institutional work at Yenching University.

1919 SPRING
Visited Baoding and Kaifeng during Spring Festival, and Taishan, Jinan, and Qufu in March.

3RD SOJOURN: 1924–1927

1924 SPRING
Married Elizabeth Pritchard Lowe, daughter of Dr. Walter I. Lowe and Catherine Caskey Lowe of Hamilton, New York, on January 18. Arrived in Beijing on March 13 to resume post as secretary of the International Committee of the YMCA. Began studying Chinese at the North China Union Language School and conducting socio-economic surveys of Chinese family life. First trip to Miao Feng Shan in April, a popular pilgrimage site northwest of Beijing.

1924 FALL
Traveled to Chengde, Lanxian, Tangshan, and Tianjin.

1925 SPRING
Traveled to Shanghai in January to meet a commission on social and economic research, and returned to Beijing by way of Qinhuangdao and Tianjin. Second trip to Miao Feng Shan with Arthur W. Hummel, Franklin C. H. Lee, and L. Carrington Goodrich in April.

1925 FALL
Taught at Yenching University, Union Medical College, and the American Women's College Club.

1925 SUMMER
Traveled to Japan to join Dr. and Mrs. Lowe, and accompanied them to Beijing, Beidaihe, and Shanhaiguan.

1926 SPRING
Conducted research on prices, wages, and the standard of living in Beijing. Gamble's first child born on March 21.

4TH SOJOURN: 1931–1932

1931 SUMMER
Returned to China for fourth and last sojourn, following a second trip to the Soviet Union. Became involved in the administration of Yenching University.

1931 FALL
Moved to Dingxian to serve as research secretary of the National Association for the Mass Education Movement, and carried out surveys of village life in northern China.

1932 SPRING
Departed Shanghai for the United States on February 23.

1933
Published *How Chinese Families Live in Peiping.*

1934–1968
Continued to publish books and articles on aspects of Chinese village and family life. Elected member of the National Council of the YMCA. Became Treasurer, Vice Chairman,

1914–1916
Worked part-time for the California State Commission on Immigration and Housing while studying for a Master of Arts degree in economics at the University of California at Berkeley. Awarded fellowship in 1915 which involved a six-month residence at the Preston School of Industry in Ione, California.

1916–1917
Taught in the economics department, University of California at Berkeley.

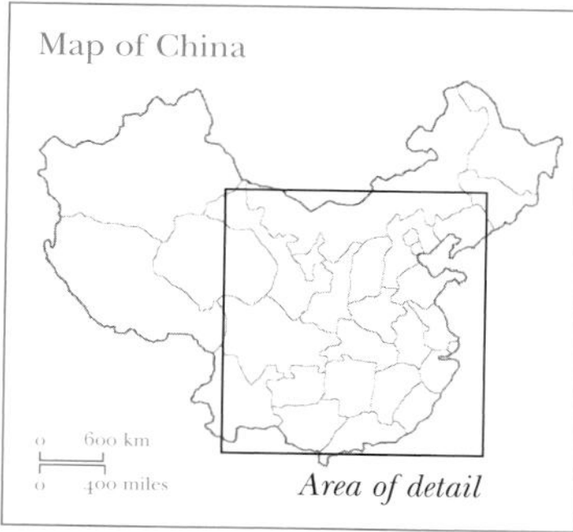

1919 SUMMER
Worked on survey materials at Beidaihe.

1919 FALL
Traveled to Hangzhou.

1919 WINTER
Returned to Pasadena, California, in December, with negatives of some 2,500 photographs taken during second sojourn.

1921
Published first book, *Peking: A Social Survey*, with the assistance of J. Stewart Burgess. Traveled as member of a commission headed by G. Sherwood Eddy to study the labor movement in England and relief work in Germany, Austria, and Czechoslovakia.

1922–1923
Prepared for third sojourn in China at New York Union Theological Seminary, New York School of Social Work, and Columbia University.

1926 FALL
Traveled for three weeks in the Soviet Union with G. Sherwood Eddy and 25 Americans, including brother Dr. Clarence Gamble.

1926 WINTER
Accompanied wife and daughter back to the United States on November 11, and stayed in Pasadena until early 1927.

1927 SPRING
Sailed for China on February 26, arriving in Shanghai on March 25; then traveled to Beijing by way of Qingdao and Tianjin. Took film footage of pilgrimage activities on a third trip to Miao Feng Shan in April.

1927 FALL
Visited Dingxian, where the National Association for the Mass Education Movement, led by Dr. James Yen, was based.

1927 WINTER
Returned to the United States.

1929
Elected President of Princeton-Yenching Foundation.

Chairman, and President Emeritus of Church World Service; Chairman of the Executive Committee of the Josiah Macy, Jr. Foundation; President and Honorary Chairman of Princeton-in-Asia.

1968

DIED in New York on March 29 at the age of 78, survived by his widow and four children: Catherine, Louise, David, and Anne.

MONGOLIA
INNER MONGOLIA
LIAONING
JII
Yellow River
HEBEI
SHANXI
Mt.Tai
SHANDONG
QINGHAI
NINXIA
HUI
A.R.
GANSU
SHAANXI
HENAN
JIANGSU
ANHUI
Yangzi River
HUBEI
SICHUAN
IBET
ZHEJIANG
HUNAN
JIANGXI
FUJIAN
GUIZHOU
YUNNAN
GUANGXI
ZHUANG A.R.
GUANGDONG
TAIWAN
Pearl River
ANMAR
VIETNAM
1
2
3
4
5
6
7
8
9
10
11
12
13
14
15
16
17
18
19
20
21
22
23
24
25
26
27
28
29
30
31
32

AREAS IN CHINA VISITED BY SIDNEY D. GAMBLE

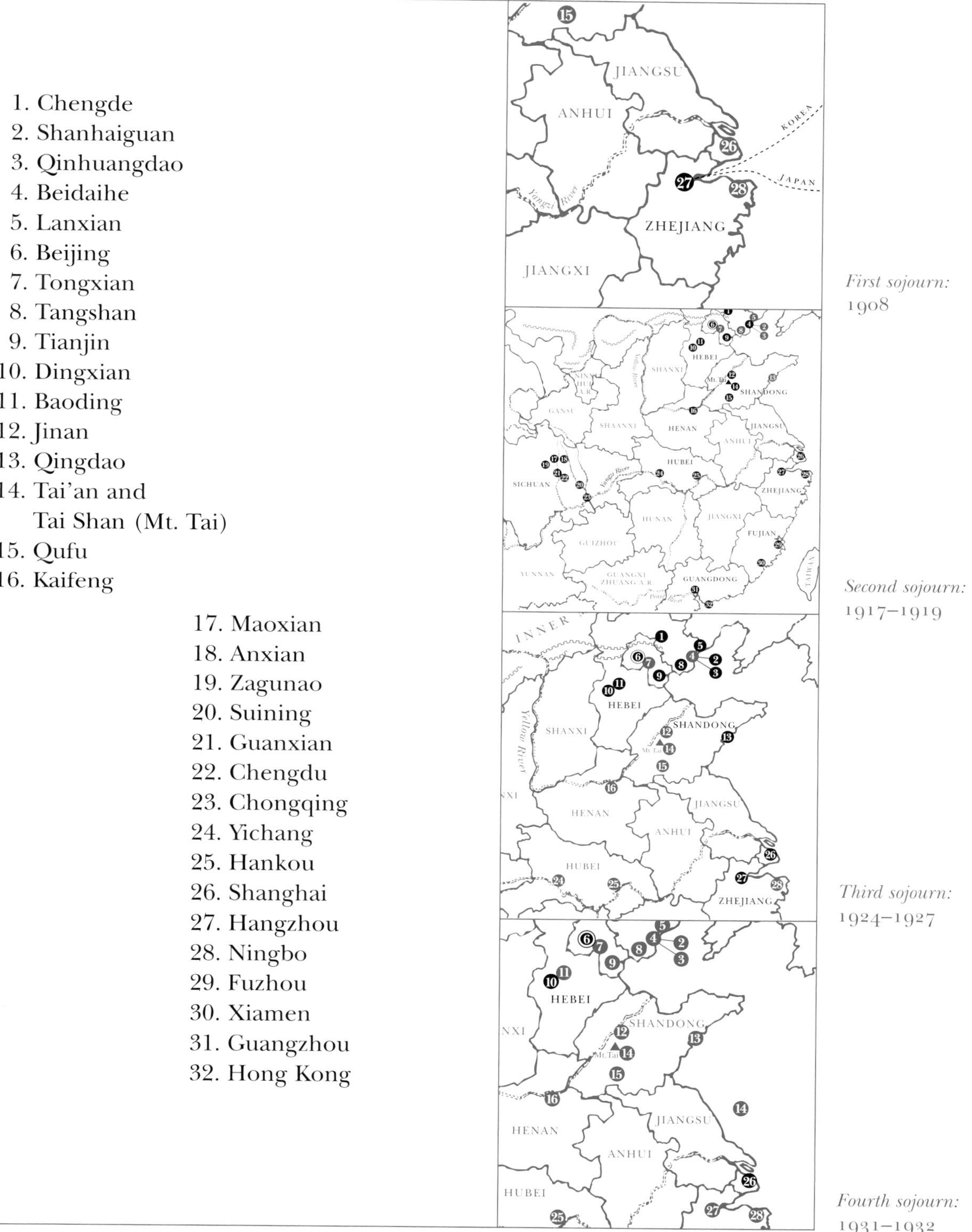

PUBLISHED WORKS:

1921
Peking: A Social Survey
New York:
George H. Doran Co.

1926
Price, Wages, and The Standard of Living in Peking, 1900–1924
Coauthored with T'ien-pei Meng
Peking (China):
Peking Express Press

1930
"Peiping Familiy Budget"
Annals of the American Academy of Political and Social Sciences 152
(November 1930):
81–88

1931
Household Accounts of Two Chinese Families
New York:
China Institute in America

1933
How Chinese Families Live in Peiping
New York:
Funk & Wagnalls

1935
"A Chinese Green Crop Society" in *Essays in Social Economics*
Berkeley: University of California Press

1943
"The Disappearance of Foot-Binding in Ting Hsien"
American Journal of Sociology 49 (September 1943):181–83

1943
"Daily Wages of Unskilled Chinese Laborers, 1807–1902"
Far Eastern Quarterly 3
(November 1943):
41–52

1944
"Hsin Chuang, A Study of Chinese Village Finance"
Harvard Journal of Asiatic Studies 8
(March 1944):1–33

1944
"A Chinese Mutual Savings Society"
Far Eastern Quarterly 4
(November 1944):
41–52

1945
"Four Hundred Chinese Farms"
Far Eastern Quarterly 4
(August 1945): 341–66

1954
Ting Hsien: A North China Rural Community.
New York: Institute of Pacific Relations

1963
North China Villages: Social, Political, and Economic Activities Before 1933
Berkeley: University of California Press

1970
Chinese Village Plays
Edited by
Sidney D. Gamble
Amsterdam:
Philo Press

OTHER AFFILIATIONS:

DIRECTOR
National Council on Religion in Higher Education

TRUSTEE
American Institute of Pacific Relations, China Institute in America, Mount Holyoke College, Riverdale Chapter of the United Nations Association, Riverdale Country School, United Board for Christian Higher Education in Asia, World University Service, Yenching University.

TREASURER
Christman Fund of Federal Council of Churches in China, Church Committee for China Relief, Far Eastern Student Emergency Fund, National Committee on Maternal Health, Riverdale Neighborhood & Library Association, World Student Service Fund.

FELLOW
Royal Geographical Society, American Geographical Society, North China Branch Royal Asiatic Society.

HONORARY DEGREES
Doctor of Humane Letters, Susquehanna University; Doctor of Laws, Hanover College; Doctor of Laws, Lake Erie College.

PAST EXHIBITIONS:

NORTH AMERICA

1989
China Institute in America
New York, NY
June 25–Sep 13

Presentation House
N. Vancouver, British Columbia
Oct 13–Nov 26

1990
University Museum
Philadelphia, PA
Mar 2–Apr 1

Hyde Collection
Glens Falls, NY
Apr 21–May 20

Wing Luke Memorial Museum
Seattle, WA
June 9–Aug 26

University of Cincinnati
Cincinnati, OH
Sep 15–Oct 14

1991
HUB Galleries
Penn State University, State College, PA
Feb 9–Mar 10

Dane G. Hansen Memorial Museum
Logan, KS
July 6–Aug 4

Columbia Museum of Art and Science
Columbia, SC
Aug 24–Sep 22

Newport Art Museum
Newport, RI
Oct 12–Dec 29

1992
Washington State University
Pullman, WA
Jan 25–Feb 23

George Mason University
Fairfax, VA
Mar 14–Apr 12

Chinese Culture Center
San Francisco, CA
June 20–Sep 6

Cornell University
Ithaca, NY
Sep 26–Oct 25

Dickenson College
Carlisle, PA
Nov 14–Dec 13

1993
Mount Holyoke College Art Museum
South Hadley, MA
Jan 9–Feb 21

Field Museum
Chicago, IL
Apr 10–June 20

CHINA AND HONG KONG

1999
The Museum of History
Beijing
Sep 16–Oct 10

2000
The Chengdu Museum
Chengdu, Sichuan
Jan 20–Feb 20

Metropolitan Plaza
Chongqing, Sichuan
Mar 29–Apr 17

Zhejiang Museum
Hangzhou, Zhejiang
May 30–June 30

Nanjing Science Hall
Nanjing, Jiangsu
July 4–25

Guangdong Fine Arts Museum
Guangzhou, Guangdong
Aug 8–28

Shenzhen Museum of Fine Arts
Shenzhen, Guangdong
Aug 31–Sep 20

Tianning Temple
Jinhua, Zhejiang
Sep 25–Oct 15

Henan Museum
Zhengzhou, Henan
Oct 23–Nov 20

Shandong Museum
Ji'nan, Shandong
Nov 25–Dec 15

2001
Hebei Museum
Shijiazhuang, Hebei
Dec 20, 2000–Jan 8, 2001

Shanghai Museum of Fine Arts
Shanghai
Jan 13–Feb 6

Tianjin Library
Tianjin, Hebei
Apr 25–May 31

2003
Heritage Museum
Hong Kong
May 3–Oct 6

S. D. G.

photographs by

SIDNEY D. GAMBLE

from 1917 to 1931

70,034 According to our count there were 70,034 families in Ting Hsien in 1931. They were living in the hsien city, 10 "towns" and 433 "villages" (TH:NCRC, P.21).

Traffic Through Gate

DINGXIAN, HEBEI 1931 Dingxian (Ting Hsien) was the principal site of James Yen's Mass Education Movement. Gamble conducted his research on rural life there, which he later published in two classic books: *North China Villages* (1963) and *Ting Hsien: A North China Rural Community* (1954).

1,524 The foreign population of Peking, exclusively of those living in the Legation Quarter, is given for 1917 as 1,524. Of these, 595 were Japanese, 281 Americans and 230 English (P:SS, P.30).

Two Men at a Table

LIFAN TO MAOZHOU 1917 Gamble's trip up the Yangzi (Yangzte) River in 1917 took him to what is today Maowen Qiang Autonomous County in northwestern Sichuan province, a region inhabited by numerous nationalities. These turbaned men probably belonged to the Qiang minority which number about 100,000.

4,289 The average density of population for the entire city is 4,289 persons per square li, or 33,626 persons per square mile. This is from 2 to 4 times as dense as the population in American cities of about the same size (P:SS, P.94).

Boy Dragging Out Coal

BEIJING 1919

Making Coal Bricks

CHONGQING 1917 Rural families made their own supply of coal briquettes, using a mixture of powered coal, dirt, and water. The mixture is formed into bricks and dried, in the open air. Briquettes tend to burn more evenly and slowly than raw coal.

32 In 1918 there were 32 banks doing business along more or less modern lines. Ten foreign banks....buying and selling of foreign exchange (P:SS, P.215).

Making Paper

BEIJING 1919 Papermaking is one of China's oldest traditional handicraft industries. Straw paper, a type of coarse paper made from rags and wheat or rice straw, was used as toilet paper.

13,500 Cash

SHIFOCHANG 1917 Round copper coins with a square hole in the center for stringing, together with silver, were the prevailing currencies in China until well into the last century. 1,000 copper coins (called cash) on a string constituted 1 *diao*. In 1917, 2,000–3,000 cash (2–3 *diao*) weighed, as Gamble noted, 90 pounds and were only worth several dollars.

4,198 The police report that in March, 1919, there were 519 automobiles, 2,222 carriages, 4,198 carts and 17,815 rickshaws in the city (P:SS, P.63).

Street Scene, Big Cart

BEIJING 1924 Animal-drawn carts with very narrow wheels were best suited to transport goods along Beijing's dusty, rutted streets. Gamble reports there were 4,198 big carts, 2,222 carriages, 17,815 rickshaws, and 645 automobiles in Beijing in 1919.

Red Thorn Apples

BEIJING 1919 Called red thorn apples by Gamble, these haws still grow on hilly ground in north China. They are high in Vitamin C and in winter are candied and eaten on a stick.

75 Peking's 75 markets are a big factor in the commercial life of the city. There are the regular food markets, big buldings filled with all sorts of meats and vegetables (P:SS, P.213).

Noodle Shop

BEIJING 1924 Wheat noodles are a staple food in north China. Small shops like this one made noodles by hand and then hung them on a line to dry.

掛麵莊
源興齋

650,000 The output of the factory amounted to some 650,000 complete uniforms a year and 330,000 single garments, half of which are padded with cotton, and half lined with sheep's wool (P:SS, P.221).

Silk Loom

HANGZHOU 1918 Hangzhou has been one of China's most important silk-producing localities since the Song dynasty (960–1279). The traditional wooden looms for weaving silk were made of beams that measured up to 15 feet long and were operated by treadles sunk into the ground beneath the weavers' feet.

10 The working day established by the Peking gilds averages 10 hours for those who are manufacturing goods, and from 12 to 14 hours for those who are selling them (P:SS, P.185).

Making Baskets

HANGZHOU 1918 Handicrafts made of bamboo were, and remain, an important part of the southern Chinese economy.

Bow Maker

BEIJING 1919 In his book *Peking: A Social Survey,* Gamble describes in detail the Beijing neighborhood Dengshikou. He visited Bow and Arrow Street where, according to him, "old time weapons were made and sold as they probably had been in this very street for perhaps a thousand years."

1,000 The Blind Gild in Peking had zero store-keepers and employers, 1,000 workers, zero apprentices, total of 1,000 members. The number of workmen to one apprentice is zero (P:SS, P.430).

School for the Blind

BEIJING 1919 The first public school for the blind in Beijing was founded in 1917 by E.G. Hillier, Esq., Manager of the Beijing branch of the Hong Kong and Shanghai Banking Corp. Hillier, who was himself blind, also devised a Chinese Braille system. Traditionally, the blind earned their living as traveling musicians and storytellers, but the 14 students at Hillier's school were taught Chinese literature, arithmetic, ethics, and how to make rattan furniture.

Winding Thread

TONGNAN 1917 People in the countryside often made their own cloth from spun cotton.

25 The Fertilizer Gild allows 15 cents for medicine in case of need, and contributes 25 cents per 100 li (35 miles) for the traveling expenses of those who are being sent to their homes (P:SS, P.198).

Straw Market

SHIFOCHANG 1917 In the countryside in Sichuan province, straw is still used along with other materials to build houses, feed animals and process manure into fertilizer.

70 The 70 apprentices slept in one large room. This gave the boys barely enough space to lie down, even when they were crowded onto two plaforms, one six feet above the other (P:SS, P.219).

Sawing Coffin Tops

TONGCHUAN 1917 Chinese who could afford the expense had their coffins made to order before their death, to ensure a proper burial would be performed when the time came. In *How Chinese Families Live in Peiping*, Gamble writes, "The coffin usually is lined with cloth or silk, and furnished with a pillow, blanket and mattress... The body is washed and dressed before it is put into the coffin. Some families dress the body in grave clothes almost immediately after death, fearing that otherwise the soul may enter the next world naked."

25,395 The number of shops and stores in the city is 25,395, while 87,721 persons are engaged in industry or commerce (P:SS, P.163).

Buying Paper Silver

ANXIAN 1917 Paper money was burned at religious observations and funerals for use in the spirit world. Here, a man is purchasing paper money folded to resemble ingots. The photograph was taken in Sichuan province, six years after the fall of the Qing dynasty (1644–1911), which may explain why the man in this relative backwater is still wearing the queue, the long braid that was the symbol of Manchu rule.

Market and Shop

SUINING 1917 A summer street scene in a town northwest of Chongqing on the Fu River in Sichuan province. The shop sign advertises traditional Chinese herbal medicines.

100 While the difference between maximum and minimum temperatures is over 100°F., the average temperature for the entire year is 53°F (P:SS, P.52).

Rickshaw Stand

BEIJING 1919 In 1919 Beijing had 17,815 licensed public rickshaws. Seven years later there were 25,877 licensed rickshaws and 70,000 rickshaw pullers. Even though competition had reduced fares to the point that rickshaw pullers could barely support themselves, rickshaws were still a relatively expensive means of transportation, because they carried only one passenger at a time. Competition also came from street cars, which were faster, cheaper, and could cover greater distances.

Steaming

AN JU CHANG 1917 In a village oil mill, soy beans are ground, wrapped in straw mats, and steamed before being pressed to extract the oil.

210,000 The local tobacco crop was estimated to be some 210,000 catties. The dried leaf prepared for smoking cost from 20 to 25 cents per catty. Cigarettes were priced from 3.5 to 6.0 cents per box of 10 (TH:NCRC, P.340–1).

Tobacco Workers

MAOZHOU 1917 Tobacco was important sideline cash crop in Sichuan province. Here, workers in Maowen Qiang Autonomous County, north of Chengdu in Sichuan province, sort and bundle partially dried tobacco leaves.

Renting Smoke

ANXIAN 1917 Expensive pipes like this were used for smoking finely ground tobacco. Patrons could thus "rent a smoke."

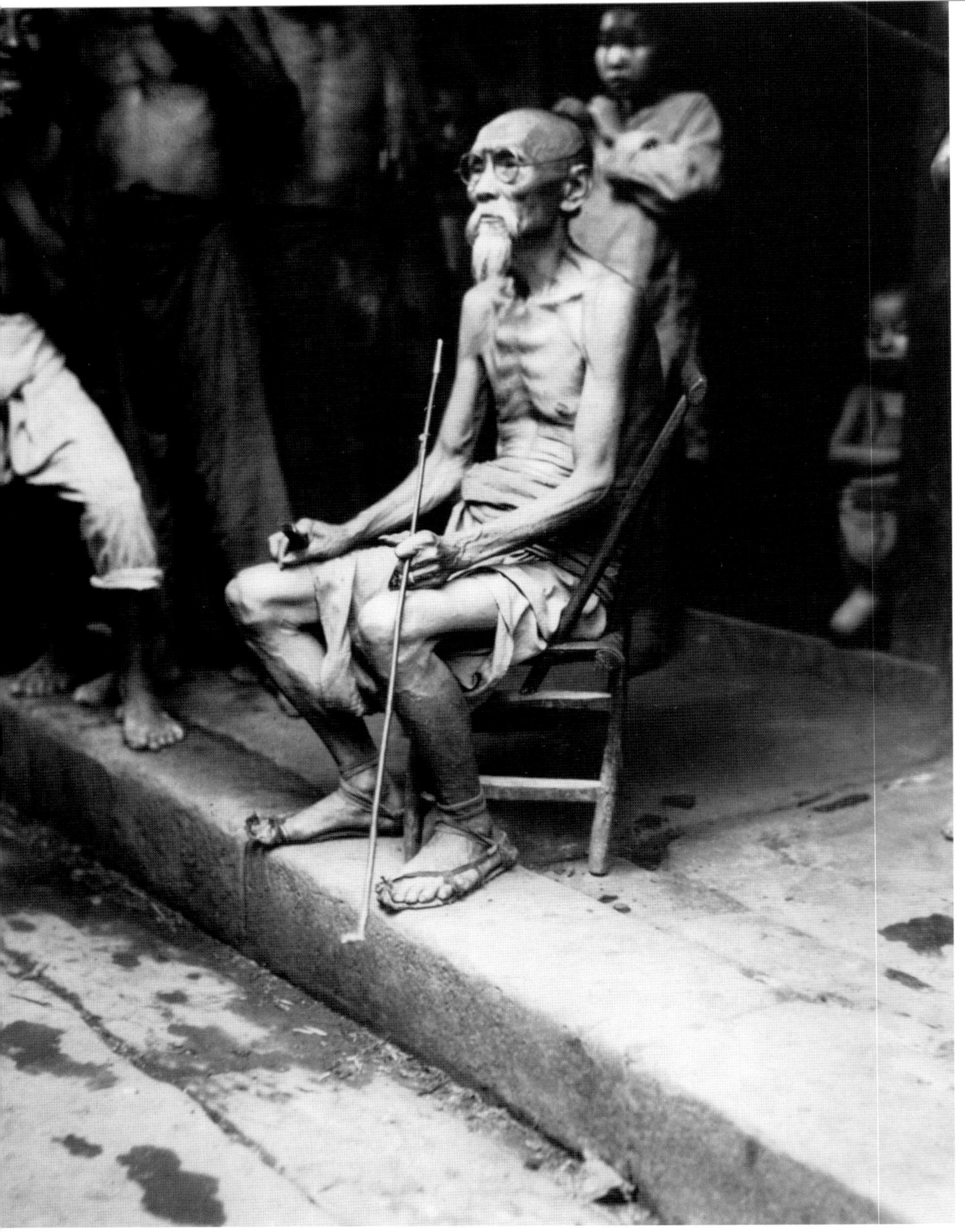

7,000 At the opium burning in October, 1919, over 7,000 ounces of opium were destroyed, while the total value of opium, morphine, pipes, needles, etc., was approximately $50,000 (P:SS, P.71).

Old Man Smoking

TONGNAN 1917 Old men sometimes owned less expensive pipes of their own.

99.2 Among the females in the 515 families who were born before 1890, and so were forty years of age or over in 1929, foot-binding was practically universal, 99.2 percent (TH:NCRC, P.47–8).

Old Lady Sitting on a Burner

FORBIDDEN CITY, BEIJING 1918 An onlooker at the presidential review held on November 13, 1918, in celebration of Armistice Day, this lady is seated on a copper incense burner. She appears to be a wealthy dowager, while the woman standing beside her might be her maid.

Old Woman

MIAO FENG SHAN 1925 Gamble noted that few women made pilgrimages to Miao Feng Shan (Marvelous Peak Mountain), yet there were women among the many beggars who flocked to the shrine during the "high season" hoping for alms from the pilgrims.

Dai Miao Pilgrims

TAI'ANFU 1919 Dai Miao, located in the city of Tai'an at the foot of Mount Tai (Tai Shan), is the chief temple dedicated to the God of the Eastern Peak.

98.8 Literacy and family income were closely related...All the families in the 100 mu and over group had at least one literate member (TH:NCRC, P.187).

So and Son

SO VILLAGE 1917 The village of So in western Sichuan province bordering on Qinghai and Tibet, was noted for its Tibetan Buddhist temple. Pictured here are So Tusa and his son, two generations of a local gentry family.

96,850 Ninety-six thousand eight hundred and fifty persons or 11.95 percent of the population of the city are listed by the police as "poor" or "very poor" (P:SS, P.270).

Man with Wine Jug

SO VILLAGE 1917 The disparity between rich and poor was noted by Gamble.

259.72 A published annual report of the Shoemakers stated that the gild received 259.72 taels, 400 cash, as rent, and 51.52 taels as interest (P:SS, P.182).

Load of Shoes

GANPU 1917 In the countryside, people wore shoes made of straw or went barefoot. Products like these straw shoes added to peasants' incomes.

Tongxian Shoemaker

BEIJING 1918 Most Chinese wore cloth shoes with soles made of cloth or rubber from discarded tires. Because cloth shoes fell apart rapidly—with exposure to rain and mud, shoemakers such as the one Gamble photographed in Tongxian (Tong county), just east of Beijing, were omnipresent.

35 The totals for 1820 years of calamities in Ting Hsien: Floods 35, Droughts 28, Locusts 21, Hail 17, Earthquakes 14, Epidemics 8, Thunder 5, Frosts 3, Pagoda 2, Snow 2, Storms 2, Boxers 1, Good years 7 (TH:NCRC, P.455).

Rowing

YICHANG 1917 The Yangzi River near Yichang (site of the Three Gorges Dam) in Hubei province. A large cargo junk might require 30–40 rowers. At certain points along the Yangzi, the currents were so swift that rowers could make no headway. Teams of "coolies" (from the Chinese word *kuli* meaning "those who do bitter work") would be hired to trudge along the river bank, hauling the boats upstream with ropes.

Man on Rope Bridge

ZAGUNAO TO BAISHUIZHAI 1917 Sometimes rope was the only way across a rapidly flowing river.

Stern River Boats

CANTON 1917 These wooden fishing boats traveled along rivers in south China where fishing was, and remains, an important part of the economy.

2,500 They [the Chinese families] secure their water from wells or from one of the 2,500 water-carriers who distribute water throughout the city in wooden tanks, mounted on big wheelbarrows (P:SS, P.31).

Water Carriers

CHONGQING 1917 The city of Chongqing, in Sichuan province, is situated on a rocky promontory at the confluence of the Yangzi and Jialing Rivers. Before water pumping stations were installed, the city relied on laborers to carry water in buckets balanced on shoulder poles.

3,439 The longest of these roads [thirteen National highways] strecthes 3,439 miles west to Kashgar in Chinese Turkestan. Others lead to Lhasa, Yunnanfu, Canton, Foochow, Hangchow, Hankow (P:SS, P.54).

Wood Market Canal

HANGZHOU 1918 Hangzhou had a network of small canals leading to the southern terminus of the Grand Canal, a 1,000 mile-long waterway built in the fifth century to transport goods between north and south China. In the thirteenth century, the canal was extended in the north to Tianjin and Beijing.

1 The general course [of the Peking Athletic Club] requires one year's study three hours a day three times a week in physiology, games, athletic drill, the use of apparatus and the science of physical education (P:SS, P.241).

Pumping Water

AN JU CHANG 1917 China's agriculture was labor-intensive and highly productive despite its low level of mechanization. To irrigate the fields, families traditionally relied on their children or hired hands—if they could afford them—to operate water wheels like this one.

Over 900 students representing all the higher schools in the city were arrested during the two days' demonstrations. More were not arrested because the government gave in (P:SS, P.78).

Student Demonstration

BEIJING, NOVEMBER 29, 1919 On November 16, 1919, when a crowd of Japanese in the southern city of Fuzhou tried to interfere with the boycott of Japanese goods, seven Chinese students were wounded. The police were called, one policeman was killed and several more civilians were wounded. As a result of this incident, Japan sent warships to Fuzhou on November 25, prompting the nationwide demonstration on November 29.

400 When the nation-wide movement started, new periodicals sprang up all over the country until early in 1920 there were over 400 of them (P:SS, P.159-60).

Sun Yat-sen Funeral Scrolls

BEIJING 1925 Dr. Sun Yat-sen, leader of the 1911 Revolution that overthrew the Qing dynasty (1644–1911), and founder of the Republic of China, died on March 12, 1925. When an important individual dies, it is customary for friends, associates and organizations to write tributes to him in black ink on white paper scrolls which are later burned. At Dr. Sun's funeral in April, the funeral committee received 7,000 wreaths, 5,900 scrolls and 500 memorial banners, all of which were later burned. A fire brigade stands ready in the foreground. Sun Yat-sen's remains were later moved to Nanjing.

京大學學生
國第二組

300,000 In 1915 when a meeting was held to protest against the Twenty One Demands of the Japanese, over 300,000 people were in the park on one day (P:SS, P.237).

Student Arrest

BEIJING, JUNE 4, 1919

Students Speaking from YMCA

BEIJING, JUNE 3, 1919 At the end of World War I, the Versailles Peace Treaty allocated Germany's former concessions in China to Japan, triggering the student movement of May 4, 1919, and a national boycott of Japanese goods. In defiance of a presidential order, university students organized speech-making contingents to promote the boycott. Here, students from a Peking University group hold forth in front of the YMCA building. On June 3, 4, and 5, over 1,000 students were arrested and detained at the government law school.

2,127 The first model prison in Peking was started only in 1909, but there are now 4 in the city with accomodations for 2,127 prisoners, while throughout China there are 39 capable of caring for 14,085 men (P:SS, P.39).

Old Style Prison

BEIJING 1918 Gamble was enthusiastic about the prison reform movement he witnessed. Old style prisons were considered dark, crowded and unsanitary by many. Here he records a "reformed" old style prison: a wooden cage 15 x 20 feet, housing 20 men. The cages were situated within walled courtyards and, sometimes, the men were permitted to leave the cages and walk around the courtyard during the day. In other cases, the men were required to wear leg shackles and to sit cross-legged.

Man and Birdcage

TIANJIN 1918 Raising birds was, and still is, a popular pastime for elderly Chinese men. Bird fanciers can often be seen at street corners or in parks exchanging advice on bird-raising.

1,169 If a person could recognize 9 characters he could read 1 out of 7 characters in simple material. 78 characters would cover 50 percent, 352 characters 70 percent, and 1,169 characters 91 percent (TH:NCRC, P.185).

North China Union Women's College Library

BEIJING 1919 The first women's college in China to grant a degree to a Chinese woman in 1909. Founded by Eliza Bridgman of the American Board Mission in 1864 as a school for beggar girls, it became the Brigman Academy in 1895 and was renamed North China Union College for Women in 1905. The college began to use the name Yenching College in 1920, when it united with three other colleges to form Yenching University—later, Peking University, or Beijing Daxue (Bei Da).

Receiving Wedding Gifts

BEIJING 1919 The two major events in a Chinese person's life are the wedding and the funeral. Even poor families would spend several months of their wages on a wedding, which represented a union of two families over time. Wedding gifts were often in the form of cash, in order to reimburse the husband's family for expenses, which typically included new clothes, a feast, a rented bridal carriage, and household furnishings. Each gift was recorded, because the couple was expected to reciprocate in the future with a gift of equal value.

Wedding Band

BEIJING 1918 Musicians leading a wedding procession, with the bride riding in a specially decorated sedan chair, on her way to the groom's home.

20,987 In 1917, there were 20,987 total deaths in Peking. 11,142 males and 9,845 females. The death rate per 1,000 males was 21.6 and per 1,000 females was 33.2 (P:SS, P.417).

Carrying Funeral Auto

BEIJING 1924 After automobiles made their appearance in China, their paper versions, like this full-sized Model A car complete with chauffeur, were integrated into the funerals of wealthy Chinese.

3 White papers folded and cut into three strips were hung outside the family gate to announce a death in the home. The papers were hung on the left side of the gate for a male, and the right side for a female (TH:NCRC, P.386).

Boys with White Wands

BEIJING 1925 White is the color of mourning in China. Leading the funeral procession out of the city to the burial ground, these boys are waving wands decorated with white paper to clear evil spirits from the path of the deceased.

3,000 Moving picture theaters have also come but recently to Peking, the first being opened in 1909....the average attendance at all the theaters being approximately 3,000 (P:SS, P.235).

Peking Lama Temple Devil Dance

BEIJING, MARCH 1919 On the twentieth day of the Lunar New Year, monks at the Yonghegong (Palace of Harmony and Concord) Temple donned costumes and masks and performed the *Dagui* (Beat the Devil) dance to exorcise evil spirits.

4 The favorite amusements of the people are interesting, in that they are a sidelight on their life. Music, reading and singing are by far the most popular amusement....Four said that their favorite amusement was talking (P:SS, P.361).

Beating Drums-Lama Monks

BEIJING 1918 Tibetan Buddhism (*lamajiao*) became influential in China during the Ming dynasty (1368–1644), under the patronage of a series of emperors. These monks are at their devotions in Beijing's best-known Tibetan Buddhist temple, the large and elegant Yonghegong. The temple was built in the early Qing dynasty (1644–1911) as an imperial residence and converted to religious use in 1745 by the Qianlong Emperor.

Taoist Priests

HANGZHOU 1918 The forms of Daoism (Taoism) range from the naturalist philosophies of Laozi and Zhuangzi to the folk practices of the monks shown here.

3 x 7 The 21st and 35th days after death were generally two special memorial days for the departed. The family, men, women, burned mourning papers and incense and wept before the tomb (TH:NCRC, P.391).

City God, Man Attendant, and Boys

ANXIAN 1917 City and town dwellers often sought the protection of the City God and erected a temple to him in the center of town. Here the City God is honored in a procession in a town in Sichuan province. The characters written on the attendant's hat read: "waiting for you."

5 The children wore a five-colored "long life string". Many boys and girls and some women wore artemesia leaves in their hair and hung "tiger" characters on their clothes (TH:NCRC, P.374).

Tiger Suit

BEIJING 1919 In China, the tiger is considered the king of animals. Thus clothing and shoes decorated with a tiger motif are popular baby outfits, as they are believed to protect the wearer from harm and illness. Gamble's notes indicate that this photograph was taken during the Dragon Boat Festival, the fifth day of the fifth lunar month.

100 The mother's family gave the bearer of the good news [of the birth] a tip of about 100 coppers and sent, by him, a return gift that was usually a basket of eggs (TH:NCRC, P.378).

Boy Smiling

BEIJING 1919

Boys Laughing

BEIJING 1924 These boys are waiting for their daily bowl of porridge at a soup kitchen (*zhouchang*), one of a dozen such establishments run by municipal authorities or charities in Beijing. One of the soup kitchens Gamble surveyed served approximately 3,000 bowls of porridge a day.

60 When a man was 60 years old and had lived through a full cycle of the Chinese calendar his family generally held a special celebration (TH:NCRC, p.379).

Bell and Stone Drums, Confucian Temple

BEIJING 1918 The Confucian Temple, located in northeast Beijing, was built during the Yuan dynasty (1279–1368). The black granite drums in the photograph may date as far back as the Zhou period (1050–221 BCE). They were discovered half buried near Xi'an in the seventh century, taken to Kaifeng in Henan province when northern China was invaded by people from Central Asia, and then transported to Beijing in 1126. The drums were placed in the temple in 1307.

EXHIBITION CHECKLIST:

Gamble Archive negative number appears in parentheses following the original title.

13,500 Cash (076A/420)
Shifochang 1917 *p.29*

Beating Drums-Lama Monks (160/897)
Beijing 1918 *p.79*

Bell and Stone Drums, Confucian Temple (204/1141)
Beijing 1918 *p.87*

Bow Maker (287/1645)
Beijing 1919 *p.37*

Boy Dragging Out Coal (540/3130)
Beijing 1919 *p.26*

Boys Laughing (456/2629)
Beijing 1924 *p.85*

Boy Smiling (529/3061)
Beijing 1919 *p.84*

Boys with White Wands (454/2616)
Beijing 1925 *p.76*

Buying Paper Silver (065A/355)
Anxian 1917 *p.44*

Carrying Funeral Auto (395/2266)
Beijing 1924 *p.75*

City God, Man Attendant, and Boys (066A/363)
Anxian 1917 *p.81*

Dai Miao Pilgrims (245/1380)
Tai'anfu 1919 *p.55*

Fortuneteller (138/778)
Hangzhou 1918 *p.III*

Load of Shoes (024B/248)
Ganpu 1917 *p.58*

Making Baskets (167/937)
Hangzhou 1918 *p.36*

Making Coal Bricks (085A/473)
Chongqing 1917 *p.27*

Making Paper (253/1424)
Beijing 1919 *p.28*

Man and Birdcage (119/671)
Tianjin 1918 *p.71*

Man on Rope Bridge (060A/329)
Zagunao to Baishuizhai 1917 *p.61*

Man with Wine Jug (51A/278)
So Village 1917 *p.57*

Market and Shop (029A/155)
Suining 1917 *p.45*

Noodle Shop (397/2277)
Beijing 1924 *p.33*

North China Union Women's College Library (307/1758)
Beijing 1919 *p.72*

Old Lady Sitting on a Burner (219/1223)
Forbidden City, Beijing 1918 *p.53*

Old Man Smoking (028A/148)
Tongnan 1917 *p.50*

Old Style Prison (240/1346)
Beijing 1918 *p.70*

Old Woman (499/2878A)
Miao Feng Shan 1925 *p.54*

Peking Lama Temple Devil Dance (237/1331)
Beijing, March 1919 *p.78*

Pumping Water (078A/432)
An Ju Chang 1917 *p.65*

Receiving Wedding Gifts (242/1363)
Beijing 1919 *p.73*

Red Thorn Apples (067B/731)
Beijing 1919 *p.31*

Renting Smoke (065A/354)
Anxian 1917 *p.49*

Rickshaw Stand (254B/1442)
Beijing 1919 *p.46*

Rowing (091A/509)
Yichang 1917 *p.60*

Sawing Coffin Tops (31A/164)
Tongchuan 1917 *p.42*

School for the Blind (254C/1448)
Beijing 1919 *p.39*

Sidney D. Gamble in Wheelbarrow (070A/384)
Xindu to Chengdu 1917 *p.VI*

Silk Loom (174A/978A)
Hangzhou 1918 *p.34*

So and Son (050A/273A)
So Village 1917 *p.56*

Steaming (079A/438)
An Ju Chang 1917 *p.47*

Stern River Boats (085A/475)
Canton 1917 *p.62*

Straw Market (077A/429)
Shifochang 1917 *p.41*

Street Scene, Big Cart (397/2279)
Beijing 1924 *p.30*

Student Arrest (261/1493)
Beijing, June 4, 1919 *p.68*

Student Demonstration (312/1783)
Beijing, November 29, 1919 *p.66*

Students Speaking from YMCA (260/1486)
Beijing, June 3, 1919 *p.69*

Sun Yat-sen Funeral Scrolls (479/2761)
Beijing 1925 *p.67*

Taoist Priests (130/733)
Hangzhou 1918 *p.80*

Tiger Suit (258/1474)
Beijing 1919 *p.83*

Tobacco Workers (062A/340)
Maozhou 1917 *p.48*

Tongxian Shoemaker (203/1135)
Beijing 1918 *p.59*

Traffic Through Gate (576/3338)
Dingxian, Hebei 1931 *p.23*

Two Men at a Table (025B/262)
Lifan to Maozhou 1917 *p.25*

Water Carriers (083A/465)
Chongqing 1917 *p.63*

Wedding Band (204/1138)
Beijing 1918 *p.74*

Winding Thread (027A/146)
Tongnan 1917 *p.40*

Wood Market Canal (167/938)
Hangzhou 1918 *p.64*